Titles b

The
Hill Barbers

Ekpe Inyang

Langaa Research & Publishing CIG
Mankon, Bamenda

Publisher:
Langaa RPCIG
Langaa Research & Publishing Common Initiative
Group
P.O. Box 902 Mankon
Bamenda
North West Region
Cameroon
Langaagrp@gmail.com
www.langaa-rpcig.net

Distributed outside N. America by African Books
Collective
orders@africanbookscollective.com
www.africanbookscollective.com

Distributed in N. America by Michigan State
University Press
msupress@msu.edu
www.msupress.msu.edu

ISBN: 9956-616-03-6

DISCLAIMER

The names, characters, places and incidents in this book are either the product of the author's imagination or are used fictitiously. Accordingly, any resemblance to actual persons, living or dead, events, or locales is entirely one of incredible coincidence.

Contents

Note from the Author

After you read or watch this play, examine the situation in your community, and if the picture is, or is close to, that depicted herein, act fast. Time and space, though often discounted, are a resource that produces or destroys every other resource.

Dedication

To Dr. Atanga Ekobo
and
Ngwene Theophilus

For their clear vision and relentless effort
to make a meaningful contribution
towards the conservation
of our rich natural heritage
in the Bakossi landscape,
a unique African forest area.

and to

WWF Sweden

For their continuous financial support to keep conservation
activities in the landscape alive.

Preface

The survival of man on earth depends on nature and its dwindling resources. Rural communities in Africa, as elsewhere, depend solely on these resources for survival. For example, in West Africa many communities depend on the forest for bush meat and other economically important resources like fruits (e.g. bush mango [*Irvingia gabonensis*]), vegetables (e.g. eru [*Gnetum africana*]), oils (e.g. from bush kernel [*Poga aleosa*] and njabe [*Baillonella toxisperma*]), traditional medicine (e.g. prunus [*Prunus africana*]), and building materials (e.g. thatches, cane rope or rattan, and timber).

The forest also helps in local (and, indeed, global) climate regulation and water catchment protection. Unfortunately, it also provides a source of land for agricultural activities, and this poses a huge problem, especially as there is rapid deforestation even in water catchments, due particularly to the traditional shifting agricultural system. In the absence of land use planning, shifting agriculture means unrestrained encroachment into fragile ecosystems, including water catchments, as land becomes scarce.

The inevitable result of the indiscriminate deforestation is acute water shortages, with obvious economic implications as a lot of time that would have been put into more productive activities is spent, especially by women and children, travelling long distances, often through the forest (a risky venture!), in search of drinking water.

The Hill Barbers depicts a community in a hilly forest landscape in Africa where farming is one of the principal economic activities. The quest for land for yearly establishment of new farms often results in land disputes, encroachment, and complete destruction of the hills (hill-

Ekpe Inyang

barbing) that serve as catchments for the community water supply. The community is almost facing the latter situation—a worst case scenario.

The play highlights the problem and effects of water catchment destruction, analysing its causes and proposing, in a subtle manner, possible measures that could be taken to address it. Although the options are left open, it is clear that the problem needs an urgent attention, as the situation is already very bad in a neighbouring community.

Ekpe Inyang

x

Characters in the Play
(In Order of Appearance)

SANGU NGOE,	an *old man, a visionary of* Mbungoe, generally addressed as Wise One
DRUMMERS,	*two masked men believed to dictate human action*
TABI,	the *greatest farmer in Mbungoe*
EYAMBE,	the *greatest hunter in Mbungoe*
YOUNG MAN,	a *playful young man who seems to predict events*
NDONGEBIDEMU NTUNGWA	the *greatest warriors in Mbungoe*
EMANGA MESAMBE	*the spokespersons of the womenfolk of Mbungoe*
WOMEN & CHILDREN	*a group that helps to fetch water in times of scarcity*

YESTERDAY

*Morning. Stage in utter darkness. Rolling of war drumbeats creates
a sinister atmosphere.*

SANGU NGOE

(Off stage.)
>   The drummers, the drummers,
>   The mystery drummers.
>   Drummers that dictate
>   The tone and pace
>   Of every human action.

(Prolonged silence.)
>   Oh, Ngoe, the venerable
>   Visionary of Mbungoe!
>   Finished are you? Too old
>   To now see clearly what lie ahead?

(A pause.)
>   What do I really see here? Darkness?
>   Yes! Nothing short of darkness.
>   I see darkness. Impenetrable darkness.
>   Gradually and systematically
>   Engulfing our forest landscape.
>   Thick, thick darkness. Alien darkness.
>   Blurring the vision of my people.
>   But persist it cannot. Cannot, cannot!

(Loudly.)
>   Away! Melt! Melt away!
>   Me-e-e-e-e-e-elt!

*Lights, revealing two masked DRUMMERS facing each other at
both sides in front of the Traditional Hall, the front wall of which
is decorated with traditional symbols, including important animals
of the forest landscape. The DRUMMERS are dressed in colourful
loincloths tied round their waists like shirts, their exposed upper*

3

bodies equally decorated in traditional makeup powder of various colours. One DRUMMER *is doing the drumming, the other waiting to take his turn. Drumming rises to crescendo, then subsides as* SANGU NGOE, *dressed in a large loincloth tied over the left shoulder, enters, stooping on his walking stick in slow reverential steps. He takes centre stage, turns round and faces the audience, wipes his eyes with his left hand and stands still, staring into space.*

A different war rhythm, rolled out by the other DRUMMER. *Enter* TABI, *dressed in very old trousers and shirt, a cutlass in the right hand, a hoe on the left shoulder. The drumbeats boil into sporadic, palpitating throbs.* TABI *looks left, right, up, down, left, right, up, down, in rhythm with the drumbeats, as he walks to stand face-to-face with* SANGU NGOE. *Drumbeats fade gradually into the background.*

TABI
Good morning, Wise One.

SANGU NGOE
Good morning, Tabi.
What treatment by the night this time?

TABI
Tormented, Wise One,
Badly tormented.

SANGU NGOE
What?

TABI
Good dreams are a rare commodity
These days, Wise One.

A brief roll of drumbeats, this time made of communicative tones.

SANGU NGOE
(Listens, then turns and faces the audience.)
>Heard that? Heard that?
>The message of the drums?
>It bears waves and beats
>Too sinister for Mbungoe,
>The quintessence of magnificent
>Splendour and bounty.

TABI
>Simple drum sounds,
>Wise One.
>Simple traditional war beats.

SANGU NGOE
(Ignoring TABI.)
>With unfamiliar undertones
>Weaving in and out
>Of the sounds you hear.
>Those other sounds
>You can't pick up
>With mere human ears.

(TABI heaves a sigh of disappointment.)
>Oh, well, it's not your fault,
>Young man. You see,
>My life is a span of wings
>Spread over two worlds
>Living side-by-side.
>This simple world of ours
>And the one that beats
>Your imagination.
>I hear sounds and see images
>Both of this corporal world
>And that beyond your reach,
>All at once.

A fresh roll of the communicative drumbeat.

TABI

The beats of….I can't just now
Recall which society.
(Staring and nodding at DRUMMER in action.)
He really is a great drummer.

SANGU NGOE

Which?

Change to another communicative drumbeat.

TABI

The one that rolled out,
So skilfully,
The communicative beats
Of that great society.
(Listens for a while.)
This one, too, is great!
Indeed, both men
Are good at the art.

SANGU NGOE

Know do you
How many drummers
Mount the battle stage?

TABI

I see two.
There are,
Indeed, two, Wise One.
I'm not blind.

SANGU NGOE

You are, indeed,
You are.
Blind like the bat
In broad daylight.

TABI

(Thoughtfully.)
    What can I say
    In self-defence?
(A short pause.)
    Wise One,
    What's the proof that I am…?
    I can see you. Everybody.

SANGU NGOE

    Probably.
(A short pause.)
    But many like you see
    Less than one-tenth
    Of the sentient, visible world
    Around them.

TABI

    But I can see
    Everything that goes on here.
    I see very clearly, Wise One.

SANGU NGOE

    You want me to prove
    You are blind, do you?
    Know you, for instance, that
    There are actually
    Four drummers on stage,
    And not just the two
    You talk about?

TABI

    But there are two.
    Only two,
    No more, no less.
(Pointing at each DRUMMER at a time.)
    One, two.

7

SANGU NGOE

The only two you can see,
The ones covered
In earthly garments.
Because you are blind
To the other world,
See you can't the naked two
Behind the two.
Deaf to that world, too,
You obviously are.

(Change again in drumbeats to a different communicative rhythm which gradually fades into the background.)

The message of the drums
Rolled out by the naked two
You certainly cannot hear.
That message is clear warning
About a terrible picture,
Picture painted
By your counterparts
On the other mountains.

TABI

My counterparts,
Seven mountains away,
Have proven their worth.
They have, within a year,
Barbed their hills clean,
Shaped their entire landscape,
Turned out loads of food.
Hardworking men they are!

SANGU NGOE

(Cynically, facing the audience.)

Hardworking, indeed,
Hardworking!

For barbing clean
All their hills in no time!

A sudden blast of drumbeats building up into those of war.
SANGU NGOE acknowledges the rhythm in a brief display.
Drumbeats die into sustained softness.

TABI
Great Hill Barbers
They really are.
And dividends of their effort
Are many and great.

SANGU NGOE
(In an imperious tone.)
Dividends are many,
But problems now follow
In torrents and floods.
The story can best be told
By women of that
Ill-fated landscape.
(Facing the audience.)
The picture, indeed, is terrible.
In simple terms,
It's an ugly sore.

TABI
(Holding his chest with the right hand, agape, head bowed.)
Ugh! An ugly sore! Ugly sore!
The picture, it makes me
Feel like throwing up,
Wise One, it really does.
An ugly sore!

SANGU NGOE

A more polite description
Of the picture that is.
Though still it does provoke
Such terrible nausea in you.
Well, it should, it should.
The truth is,
Your counterparts
Have turned the hills
Into desert-breasts.
No more milk
To feed their hungry children.
(Stares into space, looks around and sighs.)
From the look of things,
Nemesis
Is fast catching up with them.

TABI

What do you mean,
Wise One?

SANGU NGOE

Nothing at all.
(A short pause.)
Nothing!

*A different roll of drums, clearly a dirge this time. Exit TABI,
obviously frightened by the sinister response of SANGU NGOE'S.
Enter YOUNG MAN in an acrobatic display. After a while, he
dances out of the arena, waving at the two DRUMMERS, as
drumbeats die gradually into the background.*

SANGU NGOE

I wish I still wear a child's heart.
Oblivious of sounds of trouble.
Going about my business freely,

In the face of any
Disturbing events.
(Change of drumbeats, now bubbling throbs, which die down
suddenly. Facing the audience.)
To a child every sound is music,
Every group of strokes a picture.
His eyes see no trouble,
His ears hear no trouble,
Not in its painted form.

Drumbeats rise suddenly into quick, cacophonous throbs. Enter
EYAMBE and TABI from opposite directions, in wild dance.
EYAMBE, dressed in old shorts and shirt, is carrying a gun and
TABI now only a hoe, each on their left shoulders. After a while,
drumbeats mellow gradually into the background. The two stand,
looking at each other and making gestures that seem to reflect a
discussion of plans as to where to go and work for the day.

SANGU NGOE
Hey you, Eyambe! And you Tabi
Again? Where are you both going,
Bearing those weapons?
Don't you see
We face terrible weather?
Can't you see the dark clouds
Swelling and rolling in the sky?

Throb of drums that die instantly. TABI looks up, then EYAMBE .

TABI
Thick clouds of darkness, indeed.
Thick like fumes
From burning rubber.

11

EYAMBE

Emitting pungent, acidic smell,
Enough to force a giant rat
Out of its hole.

TABI

Black like soot.
Now descending upon the hills,
Upon the entire landscape.
(A pause.)
Good promise, though,
To every serious farmer.

SANGU NGOE

(Cynically.)
Good promise, indeed.

TABI

Yes, good promise, Wise One.
As rain in mighty drops
Will pour, pour, and pour
And quench the thirst
Of every dying crop.

*Change in drumbeats, now the dirge version again. TABI and
EYAMBE pace up and down, heads bowed, to the rhythm of the
drums, SANGU NGOE looking on. Sudden change in drumbeats,
now soft and near melodious, which makes TABI start dancing,
EYAMBE and SANGU NGOE looking on, arms akimbo, in
obvious dismay. Drumbeats die down abruptly.*

SANGU NGOE

You dance?

TABI

(Still dancing.)
I dance, Wise One.
Dance I must, dance, dance,
As there is real cause
For celebration!

SANGU NGOE

Rejoice do you think
We really must?
I can see you are yet to know
The music to which to dance
Or not to dance.

EYAMBE

He's dancing, Wise One,
To invite whirlwinds
And thunderstorms
To scare the animals
From my hunting tracks.

TABI

I dance to invite
Raindrops for my crops,
To feed you daily,
Give you strength
To lift your rusty, ageing gun,
The tool that makes you think not
Even of an inch of land to acquire
For your children to inherit.

*A sudden throb of war drumbeats. TABI dances in wild abandon.
EYAMBE confronts him for a fight. The two drop their weapons
and start to fight to the rhythm of the drumbeats. The fight grows
fierce, could be bloody, and SANGU NGOE dashes forward in
time to intervene to prevent an ugly scene.*

SANGU NGOE

St-o-o-o-p!
(Drumbeats subside into the background.)
What do you think
You're doing?
Haven't you noticed the sky
Displays erratic moods these days?
And, thus, can't you deduce we face
Problems stacked in sacks already?
Why dare you want to create
A new of problems
In this already tilting landscape?
Why try to
Complicate matters all the more?

EYAMBE

Wise One,
This man chops down
The forest day-by-day,
And sends the animals
Up the mountaintops,
Far, far into the heart
Of the forest. These days,
I trek miles and spend days
In the vast expanse of a forest
That's now growing so silent,
Filled with air of melancholy,
Scary to walk,
Encountering none to kill.

TABI

Wise One,
He and his men
Have turned the forest
Into a battlefield,

14

Forcing the animals into my farms,
To destroy my crops.
My family these days
I barely feed.

A sudden throb of drums, which stop instantly.

SANGU NGOE
Is that all?
Is that all you have to say,
Young men? Shame!
(A pause.)
A big shame, indeed,
That you can't see
We face far greater problems
Than those trivial, childish
Complaints of yours.

EYAMBE
It's all about survival,
Wise One. Basic survival.
How to eke out a living
From the fast dwindling resources.

SANGU NGOE
(Facing the audience.)
And by scrambling
In an effort to make that living,
Can't this man see
They're destroying
The very source
Of our own existence?
(A sudden throb of drums again.)
What we have left
Hang precariously
On a delicate balance.

TABI
What, Wise One?

SANGU NGOE
What what?

TABI
What you've just said,
Wise One.
A frightening picture it is,
If that be true.

SANGU NGOE
The truth, the truth,
The simple, naked truth.
The core of the pill,
Too bitter to accept.

Another sudden blast of war drumbeats which rise into quick, wild throbs. SANGU NGOE stoops out of stage in obvious despair. TABI steels himself against a wall, watching SANGU NGOE leave. Oblivious of what is gong on, EYAMBE takes his turn to dance to the war rhythm. Sudden stop of drumbeats. Silence.

TABI
So you, too,
Dance to this rhythm?

EYAMBE
Of course, I do.
Hard to resist the temptation
To dance to a rhythm
That's so enticing, alluring, tantalising!

A fresh blast of war drumbeats. EYAMBE and TABI engage in a display, communicating in the sign language of a traditional society.

GRADUAL FADEOUT

TODAY

Noon. A clearing in a forest area, a short distance from the village, with the two masked DRUMMERS at both sides rolling out war drumbeats. Enter TABI, carrying a cutlass and dancing to the rhythm. He is dressed in dirty, old, torn trousers and shirt. Drumbeats rise to crescendo, and TABI starts clearing a portion near the clearing. Drumbeats die down after a while, and TABI sits on the ground and places the cutlass between his stretched out legs. The war drumbeats resume softly. Enter NDONGEBIDEMU and NTUNGWA, dressed in traditional war outfits, swords held high against each other in a fighting display. TABI stands up suddenly and picks up his weapon, causing NDONGEBIDEMU and NTUNGWA to take defensive positions. He bolts out to the consternation of NDONGEBIDEMU and NTUNGWA. The sound of the war drumbeats double in intensity and speed, and NDONGEBIDEMU and NTUNGWA start fighting again to the rhythm. After a short while, the drumbeats die down, and they stop fighting, walk off in opposite directions and stand at a safe distance, facing each other in obvious anger. A sudden blast of drums, which stop abruptly.

NDONGEBIDEMU
This stretch of forest
Belongs to me.
I inherited it from
My father.

NTUNGWA
No, it is mine.
My father's father
Leased it to your father's father.

NDONGEBIDEMU
Who is older, Ntungwa,
To tell the story

Of land ownership
In Mbungoe,
You or me?

NTUNGWA

It matters not, Ndongebidemu,
Matters not at all.

NDONGEBIDEMU

(Mimicking contemptuously.)
It matters not at all.
That's what you can say.
Because you simply have
No story to tell.

NTUNGWA

Uncles, old and young have I,
In great numbers,
From father's side
To mother's side.
Their duty it has been,
From time to time,
To take me around,
Showing me boundaries
Of family land.
Huge family land!

A thunderous throb of drumbeats, and the war rhythm continues even louder and faster than before. Re-enter TABI, cutlass in hand, dancing vigorously to the rhythm.

NDONGEBIDEMU

Stop there!
Right there, Tabi!
(TABI stops instantly. Drumbeats also subside into the background.)

20

What do you think you're doing?
Inviting us to a fight?

TABI

(Obviously frightened.)
No. That's not the intention.
Not my objective here at all.

NDONGEBIDEMU

Good, then, good.

NTUNGWA

But, then, tell us, Tabi,
What brings you back here,
In this heat of day,
And in that manner,
To the battlefield?

TABI

Battlefield?

NDONGEBIDEMU

Answer as it's asked.
What are you here to do
With that weapon in hand?

TABI

(In no trembling tone.)
To mark out a piece of forest
More clearly for myself,
Like every wise farmer would.
The season's ripening fast,
And competition's
Becoming really fierce.

NTUNGWA

Wait a minute.
A piece of forest, did you say?
Which forest? Which one?
Which do you mean?

TABI

(Becoming bolder.)
Right where we stand, Great Warrior.
Right here.

NTUNGWA

Tell me you mean not
What you've said,
Fine fellow.
Tell me you're referring to
The thorny stretch
Across the turbulent river.

TABI

It's right here, Great Warrior,
Right here. See you not
Where I started clearing?

NDONGEBIDEMU

It can't be here,
It simply cannot be.

NTUNGWA

He surely is mistaken.
The landscape's changing fast,
Confusing to youthful eyes.
(To TABI.)
Go back home, young man,
And ask your uncles or aunts

To tell you the exact stretch
That is yours.

NDONGEBIDEMU

This stretch of forest,
It belongs to me, Tabi.

NTUNGWA

No, it is mine!

TABI

Mine, too, it is,
Great Warriors,
Mine!

*NDONGEBIDEMU and NTUNGWA burst into derisive
laughter and stop abruptly.*

NDONGEBIDEMU

It can't be yours, young man,
It simply can't be.

NTUNGWA

Never, fine fellow,
Not in your wildest dreams.
None of your great,
Grandparents
Dreamt of owning farms
In this part of Mbungoe.
Not even your father ever did.

*NDONGEBIDEMU and NTUNGWA burst out laughing
again. A sudden throb of drums; this grows into another type of
war rhythm. The two warriors step out in war display and suddenly
take positions at both sides of TABI'S, but a distance away from*

the latter, their swords held high as if in readiness to cut him into shreds. Enter EMANGA and MESAMBE, dressed in colourful loincloths and blouses and dancing as if invited by the drums. NDONGEBIDEMU and NTUNGWA put down their swords at once, watching the women, spellbound. Drumbeats grow softer and more melodious, and then stop abruptly. NDONGEBIDEMU and NTUNGWA swerve round.

TABI
(Loudly, confused, visibly trembling.)
> No, no, no!
> I give up the forest scramble.
> I leave it for you.
> Every square inch.
> So don't kill me.
> No, don't! A family have I
> That on me solely depends!

Enter SANGU NGOE, stooping on his walking stick.

SANGU NGOE
> I heard you from afar,
> Got all your vain
> Points of argument.
> Too acrimonious, though,
> To be totally ignored.

NDONGEBIDEMU
> Vain points, Wise One?
> You describe what transpired
> Between us as vain?

NDONGEBIDEMU and NTUNGWA look at each other and stamp out angrily.

EMANGA

I heard them, too.

MESAMBE

Me, too.

MESAMBE

This forest stretch,
To whom does it really belong?

EMANGA

I wonder.

Blast of drums. Silence.

SANGU NGOE

(After a short while, facing the audience.)
As you can sense,
A flood of problems roll in.
Like wild waves on the high sea.
There is war on our forest
At this instant.
Cold, cruel and bloody war!

MESAMBE

Wise One,
There are
More urgent problems
To worry about
Than simply
The war-on-the-forest thing
You talk about.
(A pause.)
Now we have
No water to drink.

No water to wash our cloths
And pots and plates.
Not a drop.

Another thunderous roll of war drumbeats. Exit EMANGA and MESAMBE. TABI falls out in war dance display. Enter WOMEN dressed in large flowing gowns, followed by a train of CHILDREN, each individual with an empty bucket in the hand, moving tiredly to the rhythm of the drumbeats. TABI stops dancing and stares at them in amazement. SANGU NGOE sighs and shakes his head in distress. WOMEN and CHILDREN exit from the opposite end. Enter EMANGA and MESAMBE, dancing gracefully as drumbeats mellow into pleasant softness. Shortly after, the drumbeats die down.

SANGU NGOE

(Facing the audience.)
    What have you seen?
    Hope not just the dancing to distort
    The image of the real event.
(A pause.)
    The problem's taking on
    A new dimension. And
    The burden's clearly
    So heavy on the women;
    On the children, too.
(A pause.)
    A great lesson Yesterday is
    On how Today to live
    For a certain or better Tomorrow.
    Yet refused we obviously have
    From that lesson to learn.
(A pause.)
    No forest, no water.
    Simple truth.

EMANGA

True, Wise One.

MESAMBE

But why?
Why, Wise One?
What's the link?

EMANGA

They are cutting down the trees
That cover the hills.
Like the Hill Barbers
On the other side
Of the mountain,
They are fast turning the hills
Into bare mounds of earth.
Bald like vulture heads
They soon will become.

TABI

But it is you that set
The forest in flames
At the end of the story,
Aren't you?
To you that does no harm
To the hills, eh, Emanga?
Look at the sky,
(EMANGA and MESAMBE look up rather spontaneously.)
Dark with fumes.

MESAMBE

A normal event, a normal event!
For I see nothing so particular about
Thick smoke spiralling into the sky.

EMANGA

(Looking down in disappointment.)
    A sad event, Mesambe,
    Clear pollution
    Of the air
    On which we all depend.
(A pause. To TABI.)
    Whoever told you I burn the forest
    Tells insipid lies.
    Who does not know,
    Like Grandmother,
    I rake and gather
    The grass in heaps,
    A few of which I actually burn?
(A short pause.)
    The rest I leave to rot
    And form the soil.
    Is that setting the forest ablaze?
    I have no hand in what goes on there.

MESAMBE

    Even if you had,
    Is that why
    We now lack water
    To drink and wash?

SANGU NGOE

(Facing the audience.)
    Listen, listen, listen to that.
(A Pause.)
    What a question!
    What a pity to hear
    That coming from an adult!

A blast of war drumbeats. Enter EYAMBE, his gun on the left shoulder, dancing to the rhythm. He stops suddenly as he notices the tense atmosphere. Drumbeats die into the background.

EYAMBE
Trouble, I sense trouble.

MESAMBE
Loads of trouble.

EMANGA
No forest, no water.
That's what Wise One has said.

MESAMBE
Difficult I find it still
To see the link.

EMANGA
Our hills are fast becoming bald.
Can't you guess what problem
Is likely to follow?
And the heavy burden
Is on us the women, mind you.
And our innocent, little children.

EYAMBE
My father used to tell me
The forest is store of water for us
Like mother is of milk
For her baby.
(Fixes a steady gaze at the forest clearing, and then sighs.)
The Hill Barbers,
Like this fellow here with us,
Are helping
To turn the story sore.

TABI
(Facing the audience.)

29

There he is again,
Pointing fingers at me,
Picking on me,
Criticising me.
(Turns and faces EYAMBE.)
Can you assess
The extent of damage
You yourself have so far done
To Mbungoe?
(Turns and faces the audience again.)
Now let him tell you, for instance,
Where is he going just now?

EYAMBE

Forest, of course.

EMANGA

(Anxiously.)
To do what?

EYAMBE

Hunt, I need not say.
Know you not my trade?
(Showing off his gun.)
And seeing this potent tool,
Can't you guess my mission?
(Kisses it.)
Potent tool!

MESAMBE

No forest, no animals.
And our forests are flying away
By the day.

EMANGA

And where will he be putting
That potent tool of his into use?
Which animals are there left
For him to hunt?

EYAMBE

Chimps, elephants,
To name a few.

SANGU NGOE

Where?

EYAMBE

Rock Hill.
There, at least,
Some still are left.

SANGU NGOE

Unbelievable! Incredible! Implausible!
Rock Hill?
Home of our ancestors
And land gods?
There to set your weapon?

EMANGA

(Shouting and running about, with hands on the head.)
　　　Blasphemy, blasphemy, blasphemy!
(Stands still, facing the audience.)
　　　Or what would you call it?
　　　Isn't it, indeed, blasphemy?
　　　This is clearly what
　　　Every sane mind should shun?
(A pause.)
　　　Gone insane has he?

31

MESAMBE
Rock Hill? Can't believe it!

EMANGA
Abomination!

MESAMBE
Abomination, indeed.

A blast of drumbeats. Silence.

EMANGA
Even those gripped by insanity know,
Without a second thought, that
That particular hill
Deserves to be kept sacrosanct,
Treated with reverence.
(A pause.)
No-go area it has always been to all.
Except for a privileged few
Who, of course, would face death
Should they make a trip there
With any bad intentions.
(Turns to EYAMBE.)
Do you know the animals you name
Are the no-hunt type?
Totems of the god
With seven great heads they are.

SANGU NGOE
You tell him, Emanga,
Tell him more.
And I must add,
The hill now enjoys
Double protection.

32

MESAMBE

The surrounding hills
And forests, too, I hear,
Are accorded total protection.

A blast of drumbeats that stop shortly.

SANGU NGOE

I'm proud of you, women,
Really proud of you.
For the rare display of knowledge
Of the current events
In our bounteous landscape.

EMANGA

(Facing the audience.)
Our forest has been brought
To the attention of
The whole wide world.
Mounted on stage
For everyone to view.

Dance drumbeats take sway. EMANGA and MESAMBE shoot out in gracious dance to the melody, the men clapping in encouragement of the spectacular display. After a while, drumbeats die gradually into the background.

MESAMBE

Huge cameras in great display,
During the big, big ceremony
That marked the renaming
Of our great forest.

EMANGA

And, to crown it all,
Came a strange machine,

Powerful like eagle,
Wings spinning over its head.
Equipped with cameras,
It flew over the huge expanse
Of Mbungoe.

MESAMBE

Great spectacle it was,
The wondrous flight.
Images of our rich forest
Every square inch taken.
From this angle and that.
Our forest surely will find
A conspicuous place
On the map of the world.

SANGU NGOE

Teach them, women, teach them.
School these men
Who pretend to know not
What currently sweeps
Across Mbungoe.

EYAMBE

I hear Great Leopard
And his Syndicate
Have developed
Such great interest in Rock Hill
And adjacent forests
That they've decided
To carve it away from us.

EMANGA

No, it remains here for us,
Without a fence
To separate it from us.

To continue to provide
The wonderful services
It has always done.

MESAMBE

Such as?

EMANGA

If you were a man I would
Simply rename you Thomas.

MESAMBE

I express no doubt.
Not at this point in time,
At least. Point is I simply do not know,
And would like to learn.

EMANGA

You surely are one of those
Who cook daylong,
Instead of make themselves
A useful part of those
Educative meetings by....

MESAMBE

WWF.

EMANGA

Correct! That, at least,
You've managed to learn.
So I give you some bits
Of what they've taught.
(Loudly.)
The forests are great and provide
A generous supply of
Fresh air to keep our bodies cool.

35

A steady flow of
Good drinking water
To quench our drying throats.
A natural source of
Soil enrichment.
Natural! Natural!
(A pause.)
You name the rest.

TABI

But it's clear
The new dispensation
Forbids me to extend
My farms beyond
The demarcation lines.

A pause.

EMANGA

The beauty of a woman
Lies in the style of her hair,
That of a hill
In the cover of its flora.

SANGU NGOE

Good talk, Emanga,
Well put!
(In near whisper, to TABI.)
Understood have you
The message from the woman?

TABI

Understood, Wise One,
Understood very well.
But I must add she, too,
Must play her part,

36

In practical terms,
To maintain the beauty
Of the hills.
(A pause. To EYAMBE.)
I hear you, too, are forbidden
To go there hunting,
From this day henceforth.

EYAMBE

(Facing the audience.)
Then to the farms I now must go.
There to hunt the rodents
That pest his crops,
Or the men and women
That nurse and tend them.

TABI

I've doubted not your position
As great enemy of mine.
(A short pause.)
Sheer jealousy, sheer jealousy, indeed!
Because I lay claim to virgin land,
You to a rusted, ageing gun.

EYAMBE

(Casts TABI an angry look.)
I have listened to you speak,
I have watched you carry out
Your activities day after day,
And my conclusion is that you care not
About the state of our forest.

TABI

(Cynically.)
I can see you are someone that cares.

SANGU NGOE
No time for all that, young men,
No time for ranting! We need to think
Seriously about these problems.
Huge storms and floods await us
Should the trend continue.

TABI
You frighten us, Wise One,
You really do.

SANGU NGOE
So clear are the premonitions,
Though to them no one pays attention.
But I tell you, simply,
What I see coming.

A blast of drums which boil into a war rhythm. SANGU NGOE walks out, leaving EYAMBE and TABI spellbound.

GRADUAL FADEOUT

TOMORROW

Afternoon. In front of the Traditional Hall. Masked DRUMMERS still flank the stage, rolling out an enticing melody. SANGU NGOE stands still, staring into space, apparently pensive. Enter TABI, EYAMBE, EMANGA and MESAMBE, dancing to the rhythm. They stop suddenly, as the rhythm subsides, and start discussing, inaudibly amongst themselves as they find SANGU NGOE in that stationary position.

SANGU NGOE

(Deep in thoughts.)
  Listen to the heartbeat
  Of the Clock of Nature,
  The erstwhile unfailing timer
  Of natural creatures and events.
  So irregular, unpredictable, unreliable.
  Sometimes too fast, sometimes to slow.
  Certainly faulty she is, due to incessant
  Wild vibrations and shocks
  From treacherous human acts.
(A pause.)
  Far on the horizon, see what they do?
  Suffocating are they Mother Earth
  With fumes of impunity...and greed.
  And now natural events,
  How erratic they've become!
  Rains when sunshine we expect,
  Sunshine when rains we anticipate.
  Thus natural creatures assigned
  To tend and nourish Mother Earth
  Are by waves of confusion struck.
  Uncertainty prevails!
  Their roles they no longer can perform
  With poise, dexterity and confidence.

The rhythm changes suddenly to that of war, and TABI, EYAMBE, EMANGA and MESAMBE start dancing round SANGU NGOE who remains still like a statue. Enter NDONGEBIDEMU and NTUNGWA, dancing wildly to the war beats. TABI, EYAMBE and the two women stop dancing. Suddenly NDONGEBIDEMU and NTUNGWA also stop dancing. Drumbeats die down abruptly. Everyone walks slowly backward, away from SANGU NGOE, stands and takes a good look at him.

NDONGEBIDEMU

(In near whisper.)
> An unusual event! Really weird!
> Doubtful if Sangu Ngoe is still alive.

NTUNGWA

But he stands.

TABI

> Yes, he stands,
> And so he's still alive.

EYAMBE

> He stands,
> But in too still a manner
> To believe he still shares
> This land with us.
> Like a pillar of salt!

(SANGU NGOE moves his head slightly and takes a look at EYAMBE and then at TABI.)
> Oh, he still moves!

TABI

> Yes, he does.

SANGU NGOE

(Suddenly and forcefully.)
Yes. Still full of breath is Ngoe.
Strong and kicking he still is.
And has he for you a word of caution.
The destruction you now must stop.
(A pause.)
The picture of the landscape
Just three mountains away,
What ominous colours it casts!
Such an alien picture
Must here be painted not!

EMANGA

No, no! Not if we all must continue
To live happily in this land.
(A pause.)
The picture's really crazy and sore.

MESAMBE

Indeed! And laced
With ugly scars.

EMANGA

And, clearly, that alien picture's
Already taking form here
In our very bountiful landscape.

TABI

God forbid!

EMANGA

But it's true.

EYAMBE

True?

41

MESAMBE

True.

EMANGA

And the burden's already
On us the women;
Our children, too.

(Loudly.)

We really must stop
The destruction, Wise One.

MESAMBE

At once, at once!
The time is now.

SANGU NGOE

Nemesis soon
May catch up with us, too,
If the destruction
You hesitate to stop.

(A pause.)

Ndongebidemu, Ntungwa,
The great warriors of Mbungoe,
A crucial role have you
In this clarion call to play.

NDONGEBIDEMU

Yes, fight we must, fight, fight.
Fight to stop the destruction.

TABI

If stop it we really must,
How, then, shall we produce
Food enough to feed
Our swelling village? How, then,

Will some of us generate income
To address the myriad domestic
Problems we face? How?

SANGU NGOE

(Facing the audience.)
There is some sense
In what he says. But, take note,
Food production hinges not
On relentless forest destruction.

TABI

Forget you not, Wise One,
That ours is the type of soil
That gives up after a season
Or two of receiving the hack
Of the hoe. So we move on.

SANGU NGOE

True, Tabi, true.
I watch you doing that
Every single season.
Moving on,
Wreaking more and more havoc,
As the soil soon fails to respond.
Because your heads and hands
Have failed to work together
To give it proper tending.

EMANGA

True, Wise One, perfectly true.
My mother and her line of sisters
Grew up happily fed
By Grandmother
Who, year after year,
Turned the soil

Of a single piece of land,
A whispering distance
From the village.

TABI

Known is the story too well
Of the force behind
The yields she had.
Or forgotten have you
The story so soon?

EMANGA

Yes, they gave her names,
Which you have maintained
And now turned into a kind
Of song. Lazy woman, empty beauty,
The great witch that drew soil....

MESAMBE

Let's not get entangled
Into that baseless, age-long story
And digress from what's at stake.

TABI

But indolent she really was.
Lazy to toil on virgin land,
Which was why her husband,
A man known to have loved her
So well,
Went in for a second wife.

EMANGA

What about the third
He took and later dumped?
What justification, too?

MESAMBE

Exactly. What justification?
And, by the way,
On whom did she ever depend
To feed her train of children?

EMANGA

Ask him, my friend,
Ask him again.
Who fed her numerous
Children for her?

A sudden blast of drumbeats which die down abruptly after a short while.

EYAMBE

Without the least intention
To take sides, I must stress,
Without fear or favour,
The woman was, indeed,
A great witch.

TABI

Absolutely.

EYAMBE

For how on earth
Could she have been that lazy,
Wallowing on a single piece of land
Year after year,
And yet producing
Incredible quantities of food
To feed her battalion of children?

*Shaking his head disappointedly, SANGU NGOE walks away
from TABI and EYAMBE, stands at a safe distance and looks on
in total disgust.*

TABI

Is it not known she planted
A strange kind of shrub
All over the overworked plot?
Magic shrub that drew fertile soil
From every farmer's farm
To her farm to feed her crops,
While those of other farmers
Starved and grew pale or withered.

EYAMBE

Magic shrub, indeed.

TABI

Witches' siphon.
Bought from distant land.

SANGU NGOE

(Angrily.)
But that is not true!

EMANGA

(Bursts out crying amidst a dirge-like sound of drumbeats. Immediately, MESAMBE holds her tight, whispering into her ear and tapping her back as she tries to pacify her.)
Grandmother, hear that again.
Hear what your name
Has become.
The witch that drew
Fertile soil
From other farmers' farms.
Then it was a lie
Your daughter told me
You brought the shrub
From a village where

46

Every farmer planted it
Around their farms
To increase their yields.
So it was truly a lie, eh?
And does it also mean
Every farmer in that village
Was a witch or wizard?
And from whose farms
Did they draw fertile soil
To enrich their farm plots?

A pause. SANGU NGOE starts walking towards EMANGA
who has refused to be consoled by MESAMBE.

NTUNGWA

(Facing the audience.)
Something tells me
There is a lesson
We've refused to learn
From that woman's story.

SANGU NGOE

(Taps EMANGA on the back a couple of times.)
Stop crying, Emanga, stop crying.
(A pause.)
The vicious noises of false rumours
Constantly spread by man,
If harnessed in a canister
And channelled through a barrel
Directed back at the very source,
Are a bomb powerful enough
To blast and +crush this earth,
And every creature that on it crawls,
Into their primordial form of dust.
(A blast of drums.)

47

Witchcraft or magic it is
When too complicated is an art
To be understood or practised
By an overwhelming majority,
A majority that has refused to learn.

A blast of war drumbeats. NDONGEBIDEMU and NTUNGWA fall out in war display. Shortly, the drumbeats mellow into the background. SANGU NGOE gives a loud sigh of disappointment. Prolonged silence.

NTUNGWA

Something tells me
If every farmer in this land
Used the magic shrub
We would not have engaged
In this endless battle.

NDONGEBIDEMU

Absolutely. We would not be
Standing here,
Flexing our muscles
And beating our chests
Like demented mountain gorillas.

NTUNGWA

In fact, we would not have
Destroyed the surrounding
Forests and resorted to this
Barbing of the hills.

EYAMBE

But is there any shrub known
To add fertility to the soil?

NDONGEBIDEMU

That seems to be the case.
Except if we must continue to cling
On to your vain argument
About witchcraft.

TABI

But how do we
Now get that shrub,
So we can the ugly picture transform,
And the terrifying story reverse ?

MESAMBE

(In near whisper.)
Have you heard that?
He's asking for the shrub,
The very same shrub they reject.

EMANGA

(Now quite sober.)
I suspect it's not the type
They condemn.

MESAMBE

Perhaps, I didn't get him well.
(To TABI.)
Do you mean the shrub you've
Been condemning just now?

EMANGA

It can't be the same shrub
For which he now asks.
Nothing can push him
To ask for it now.

EYAMBE

There's nothing wrong in asking for it,
Especially as we now face
This terrible flood of
Life-threatening problems.
(A pause.)
The animals are
Fast disappearing,
As the forests
Are being converted to farmland.

TABI

And as the animals
Are constantly confronted
With hot cartridges and bullets.

EYAMBE

A kind of hit-back, Tabi?
When I had just been putting up
A strong defence in your favour?

TABI

(With subservient alacrity, hands raised as sign of having surrendered.)
No, Eyambe, no! No, no!

EYAMBE

Alright, then. Give me time
To drain my pipe. The problems are
Not as simple and manageable
As they appear.
(A short pause.)
Come to think of the current problem,
For example.
Are we going to survive the acute
Water shortages this time?

(A pause.)
> All because every dry season
> The hills are brutally barbed
> And our streams and rivers
> Are left naked under the hot sun.

EMANGA

(Fanning her body with the hand. Everybody follows suit rather spontaneously.)
> And there is heat, heat, heat!
> Too much heat! Strangely unbearable!

SANGU NGOE

> An unprecedented phenomenon, indeed.
> I hear they call it global warming.
> Clearly, a global warning,
> A human-induced problem,
> With promise of more serious
> Life-threatening events.

EYAMBE

> I have the feeling, Wise One,
> That the current stream of heat
> Is due to the wanton destruction
> Of our forests. *(…)* I also think that
> This acute water problem is
> Not unconnected
> With the scourging heat.

SANGU NGOE

> You are right, Eyambe.
> That's one of the causes…And….

MESAMBE

> Glad to hear this
> Coming from one of the men.

51

For they've always been so callous
And indifferent whenever there are
Discussions about these problems.
(In a sudden realisation, to SANGU NGOE.)
I'm sorry, Wise One,
For the somewhat rude interruption.

SANGU NGOE

That's all right, Mesambe, alright.
Good it is to speak out, in clear terms,
When problems we perceive swelling
And mounting by the day.
(A pause.)
Today experience we climate change,
A warning we must our ways
Radically mend,
Allowing nothing to chance.
(Silence. Paces up and down, and then bursts into occasional emotional outpours, facing the audience intermittently.)
Indeed, to look at the problems,
Using a global lens,
Is to make yourself even more sick.
(A pause.)
Knowledge of what man now does
To Mother Earth,
And the negative impacts
On natural systems, drives me mad.
Drives me mad, my own people,
That knowledge drives me really mad.
(A throb of drums.)
I wish I were ignorant.
Ignorant enough like the lamb
For burnt offering grown.
For ignorance spares one the trouble
To worry about the inevitable

Concomitants of one's actions.
But, mind you, ignorance is lethal.
(A pause.)
     Has anyone here ever paused,
     For just a moment, to ponder
     On the harm we cause to Mother Earth?
     There she remains still,
     Lying like any good nursing mother,
     With her breasts of bounty
     Left open for us to feed from freely,
     Despite the frequent, painful bites
     On the sore nipples.
(A throb of drums.)
     Her we surely see
     More like a giant whale
     On our seashore of greed.
     A helpless organism,
     A free launch for the greedy!
(A pause.)
     But think we no pain she feels,
     When daily from her we siphon
     Not only gallons of milk
     But barrels of pure blood?
     Think we no pain she feels,
     When daily from her we scoop out
     Not only pounds of flesh
     But also peel off hectares of skin?
     All for our egos to satisfy!
(A brief display of war drumbeats.)
     Well, no cause for alarm,
     Were it not that the deep wounds
     That on her we've wantonly created
     Are given not the least time to heal
     Before fresh wounds into her again
     We dig and dig and dig.

(A short pause.)
>All this only for our lives to sustain?
>No. Surely for our egos to gratify.
>For our personal aggrandisement.

(A brief display of communicative drumbeats.)
>Well, true. True, indeed.
>Human it is to struggle
>For wealth to amass
>And rich to become
>For power to gain.

(A short pause.)
>But short of expediency it is
>To do so to the detriment
>Of the health
>Of Mother Earth.

(Another brief display of communicative drumbeats.)
>But no, continue it cannot forever;
>For on her we all depend,
>Everyone of us.
>On her we crawl like tiny ants
>On a mighty ship on sail,
>A ship afloat the turbulent sea of space.
>Yet on her we daily create
>Huge craters of gores
>With massive chisels of greed.
>So deep now are the holes
>She, sooner or later, might sink.

(A blast of drumbeats.)
>She bleeds, she bleats,
>She groans, she moans
>In severe pain and agony.
>Her heart palpitates and trembles
>With fear of impending doom,
>Of looming catastrophe,
>Of imminent death.

(A brief dirge-like roll of drums.)

54

Sick she really is.
Yet on her we daily throw
Loads of pollution of all species.
(A pause.)
She sneezes, she wheezes,
She coughs, she's choking.
For time we give her not
To clean up the suffocating mess.
Now she's with high fever struck.
(A brief display of war drumbeats.)
And now, like greedy ants
On an oily frying pan on fire,
We're gradually being trapped
By this unprecedented upsurge of heat.
Heat too frightening, too horrifying,
Too terrifying to permit
Even a moment's tranquil sleep.

Another brief display of communicative drumbeats. Erie silence.

MESAMBE

(In near whisper, to TABI.)
Heard it, what Eyambe gave,
And now Wise One presents,
As causes of the excessive heat?
And of water shortages?
(TABI turns his face in the opposite direction.)
Now *w*omen, including your wife,
And children bear the brunt.

EYAMBE

The soils, too, are becoming
Poorer and poorer, as they are
Frequently burnt and overworked.

MESAMBE turns her face in obvious guilt.

55

NDONGEBIDEMU

True, perfectly true.
And fingers point
At you the women.

EMANGA

Not me. Please, keep me out of it.
Completely out of it. Blame, like credit,
Should go only to whom it is due.

NTUNGWA

You may be the only exception.
For, in fact, the womenfolk
Has helped to destroy the soils.

NDONGEBIDEMU

Women are, indeed,
The relentless engineers
Against soil rejuvenation.

EMANGA

And men the engineers
Of the growing land disputes
And unending deforestation.

NTUNGWA

What are you up to, Emanga?
Accusing Great Warriors
Who've fought so hard to secure
The forest we now all enjoy?

EMANGA

But you've been accusing....

MESAMBE

(Interrupting, to EMANGA.)
> You remember, my friend,
> The shrub? The magic shrub?
> I clearly have forgotten
> The name of that shrub.

EMANGA

Magic Shrub, Mesambe,
Simply Magic Shrub.

TABI

No, no, no. That's not the name.

EMANGA and MESAMBE look at each other, burst into derisive laughter and stop shortly. NDONGEBIDEMU and NTUNGWA walk a short distance away and engage in an inaudible conversation.

EMANGA

> Well, well, well. I see,
> It's not just
> Magic Shrub, my friend,
> It is Witches' Siphon.

MESAMBE

(Even more cynically.)
> Exactly. And there's
> Nothing wrong with men asking
> For Witches' Siphon.

TABI

(Apparently absentmindedly.)
> Nothing wrong at all,
> Mesambe, nothing wrong.

EMANGA and MESAMBE look at each other again and burst into an even louder derisive laughter.

NDONGEBIDEMU
Stop, women, stop.
Stop these silly, teasing jokes.

NTUNGWA
But these men have refused to act
Like gentlemen by starting such a topic.
And, thus, they should,
In order that they learn and behave
Properly towards women thereafter,
Be left to taste the ridiculing
Tinge of the female avenging tongue.

NDONGEBIDEMU
But not at this trying moment,
My friend, not now.

A sudden throb of drums, then silence.

SANGU NGOE
I see, I see.
(A pause. Facing the audience.)
You see, though quite stubborn
And adamant can some men be
Especially when your ideas
Synchronise not with theirs,
Known are they also to learn
And act fast in circumstances
When the wheel of things
Seems grinding to a halt.
(A short pause.)
As you can sense,
There's a marked change

In the collective psyche at this instant.
And the current predicaments
Are reason enough
To push even the lame
Jumping into spontaneous action.

A sudden blast of dance drumbeats. EMANGA and MESAMBE dash out and start dancing gracefully to the rhythm, the men clapping their hands. There is a sudden change to war drumbeats, and the two women leave the dancing arena as NDONGEBIDEMU and NTUNGWA jump in. The drumbeats die abruptly into the background.

NDONGEBIDEMU
We must stop the destruction now,
Whatever it takes, now!

NTUNGWA
Stop it we must without looking
Behind our shoulders.

EYAMBE
We must stop it at once.

TABI
At once, indeed, at once.
The present call for action
Calls for no procrastination.
(Facing the audience.)
You, you, me, we, everyone
Must stop the destruction now.

SANGU NGOE
(Who has remained pensive all this while.)
But how?
Just how do we stop it?

(A pause.)
> Or should we send the warriors out
> To punch and pound and batter
> Anyone found defiling
> Rock Hill, other hills,
> And contiguous forests?

TABI

Yes, Wise One, yes.

EYAMBE

Yes, yes, yes, Wise One!

SANGU NGOE

No, no, no, young men,
No! Such a measure,
At this early minute,
Might be misinterpreted
As too radical. Rash. Brusque.

TABI

No, Wise One, No.

A sudden throb of drumbeats which gradually build into a war rhythm. Enter YOUNG MAN, striking a metal gong in harmonious blend with the drumbeats, imitating a village-crier making an important announcement. SANGU NGOE fixes a gaze at him. YOUNG MAN exits at opposite end of stage. Drumbeats suddenly fade into the background.

SANGU NGOE

(Thoughtfully, facing the audience.)
> What could this mean?
> A mere child's display?
> Doesn't seem like it. Not at this time.

For clearly I can see
There's some adult in the child.
(A short pause. In a sudden outburst.)
Yes. In what he does I see
A mature hint on a measure to take.
Yes, an injunction we must pass
Immediately, to put a definite stop
To the current wave of destruction.
Possibly accompanied
With a powerful traditional oath.
(A pause.)
Indisputably, this would hurt many.
(More loudly.)
But no choice have we, no choice.
An aggressive measure such as this
Must necessarily now be taken,
Or else the worst phenomenon we face,
The picture of which I consider
Too hideous, heinous and fearsome
A taboo for public description to give.
For by so doing it could many
To their graves send,
Much, much before their destined time.
(A pause.)
My intention it is not
In you to instil fright,
Ladies and gentlemen.
Not my intention at all.
For simply do I describe
What I see approaching.
(Gazes into space, then looks down with a sigh.)
I know for sure some might this idea
Ferociously fight against. Yes, I know.
(A long pause.)
A few seasons ago,
I saw the sunshine of

Clear hope on the horizon.
Ready to descend upon our hills.
But our persistent, cruel activities
Held it back,
Pushed it far, far away,
Inviting but these
Thick, dark,
Omen-bearing clouds.

A blast of drums that stop abruptly.

TABI

We must act at once,
Wise One, at once!
We must stop the destruction.

SANGU NGOE

But how?
(A short pause.)
Just how do we,
Indeed, stop it?

TABI

You owe us the answer,
Wise One, you certainly do.

SANGU NGOE

(In feigned anger.)
Did I the problem cause? Did I?
Why expect you the answer from me?
(A pause. Gives a broad smile.)
I see. So when devastating
Thunderstorms and floods
You and your counterparts invite,
Old Sangu Ngoe it is

That must be called in to bear
And brave the risks to stop
The dangerous, natural events, eh?
So it is he who no longer can tell
The weight of a cutlass, or an axe,
It is he that must now pay the price
Of your wanton forest destruction, eh?

EMANGA

(In near tears.)
Help, Wise One,
The situation is bad. Help!
Save our land
From this never-ending
Flood of problems.

MESAMBE

(Already weeping.)
The weight is too much on us
The women, Wise One.
The situation is getting worse.
Help! Save the land.

EMANGA and MESAMBE are now weeping loud and clear.

SANGU NGOE

Sorry, women,
For throwing you into
Such an emotional state.
(In a sudden outburst.)
But, oh, most scathing tongue,
Find no respite at this instant.
Rebuke, reprimand, castigate! Do it!
For many are becoming far too careless.
Careless, careless, careless debtors.

(A short pause.)
> Toy they with the future,
> Eat they mindlessly
> Into our common borrowed capital,
> Giving it no breathing space
> For interest to yield
> So in a better position we're placed
> For this debt to pay,
> A debt that has so continued to swell
> From generation to generation
> Of voracity, avarice and greed.

EMANGA

What, Wise One?
What debt?
I owe no one a might.

SANGU NGOE

Understand you may not;
But a universal truth it remains
That debtors we have been
Right from that moment
When the first deep breath we took,
As acceptance of our sojourn
On this living ball of dust.

(A pause.)
> Debtors of our children,
> Born and yet unborn;
> Debtors of the future
> Which from them we borrowed.

(A short pause.)
> The debt today we enjoy,
> Often so lavishly,
> Wastefully and mindlessly,
> Is borrowed capital,

The future
We've taken as revolving loan
From our children,
Born and yet unborn.
(In an almost imperious tone.)
To them the future really belongs,
Our debt to them,
Which we all must pay back
In the selfsame value
As we borrowed it, or higher.
(A pause.)
Started, though, have we
The debt to pay.
By the care and tending
Our children already born we give.
But a tiny bit of the debt
That really is,
And the part remaining
Heavier and heavier on us grows,
As deeper and deeper
Into the capital we devour.

EMANGA

(In a lamenting tone.)
Take the weight off
The women's shoulders,
Wise One.

MESAMBE

Save us, Wise One, save us.
Have pity on us.

EMANGA

Save the poor, suffering women,
Wise One, from the bitter experience.

SANGU NGOE
Heard you I have, women.

EMANGA
It is only you can intervene
At this moment, Wise One,
To save our land.

SANGU NGOE
Heard you, indeed, I have, women.

EMANGA
The situation is really, really bad!

A blast of drums that stop abruptly. Silence.

SANGU NGOE
(Facing the audience.)
     Well, ladies and gentlemen,
     See I already a clear hint
     On potential solutions.
(To TABI, EYAMBE and the others.)
     Play you well your part,
     Think the problem through
     For practical solutions.
     And mine will I play, to live or to die,
     To dismantle the forces behind
     The destruction of the base
     Of the very resource
     On which our lives depend.

NDONGEBIDEMU
You play your part to live
And not to die, Wise One.
We are here to protect you.
With all our might!

66

NTUNGWA

Nothing happens to you,
Wise One,
Not when we're around.

SANGU NGOE

(Facing the audience.)
I wish they could stand it
When it strikes.

NDONGEBIDEMU

Trust us, Wise One, trust us.

NTUNGWA

We are here to protect you,
Wise One, we are here for you.

A pause.

SANGU NGOE

(Smiles quizzically.)
You won't understand.

Drumbeats rise gradually into crescendo. NDONGEBIDEMU and NTUNGWA shoot out in a wild acrobatic display, in rhythm with the war beats. Everyone but SANGU NGOE claps their hands as they watch the spectacle. SANGU NGOE remains still, casting angry looks at DRUMMERS. Then he starts to walk away from the clapping crowd, shaking his body vigorously as he tries to extricate himself from the hypnotising forces of DRUMMERS' who have sensed his intention. This gives the impression he has joined NDONGEBIDEMU and NTUNGWA in the war display, and the crowd, except EMANGA, claps even louder, ululating.

EMANGA

(Loudly, dashing out of the crowd.)
> But no. No! No!

(Drumbeats die into sustained softness and ululation stops. But SANGU NGOE continues dancing wildly.)
> Why do we stand here
> Clapping and ululating?
> Can't we sense something foul?

(Looking at SANGU NGOE.)
> Look keenly at
> The way he displays.

MESAMBE

> Indeed, indeed.
> Like one manipulated
> By some strange force.

EMANGA

(In a lamenting tone.)
> Let's turn to God! Let's turn to Him.
> Now! Now! Now! God save us!
> Save us! Save us! Now! Now...!

(A sudden and brief throb of drums.)
> Oh, Heavenly Father,
> Most merciful Lord,
> The giver and taker of life,
> The Alpha and the Omega.
> Let the sun take down with it,
> As it now descends upon the hills,
> All the destructive, old practices
> That now are a source of doom for us.

MESAMBE

> Amen.

68

EMANGA

Let those dangerous practices
Be buried away in the deep, deep valley
Beyond, where no one can reach,
Trace and bring them back to this land.

MESAMBE

Amen.

EMANGA

Let a thick blanket of darkness,
A fearsome, gaping abyss, or
An awesome catacomb,
Appear between us
And the dangerous practices
That now ravage and mortify our land.

MESAMBE

Amen.

EMANGA

In Jesus' name.

MESAMBE

Amen.

EMANGA

In Jesus' name.

MESAMBE

Amen.

EMANGA

In the name of Jesus Christ.

MESAMBE

Amen.

A pause.

EMANGA

(Getting more hysterical.)
        Oh, Jesus! Oh, Jesus! Lord of Lords!
        Our only Saviour and Redeemer.
        Our only source of hope. Come down.
        Come down. And rescue. Rescue us.
        We need you now. Now! Now! Now!
(Pointing at SANGU NGOE.)
        There he is. There! Entangled! Trapped!
        In a web...A web...A strange web.
        Extricate him...from that web.
        From that web. Extricate him.
        Extricate! Extricate! Extricate him.
        O-o-o-h, Je-e-e-esus! Rescue us.
        Rescue us. Him. Him. Rescue him.
        Let there be hope. Peace. Harmony.
        No more destruction. No more....

Drumbeats build up into wild crescendo immediately. Ululation again, this time much louder, ostensibly in response to the supplication but obviously as SANGU NGOE continues with the wild dance, gyrating. Suddenly he staggers dangerously, pounds his walking stick on the ground rather inadvertently, and gives a loud scream instantly.

SANGU NGOE

N-o-o-o-o-o-o-o! No!
(Sudden stop of drumming. Addressing the crowd, gasping and pointing at DRUMMERS with his walking stick angrily as he does so.)
        These men,
        Their drumbeats dictate
        The tone and pace

Of your activities. But resist
The temptation to dance
To their luring tune.

(DRUMMERS cast quick glances at each other in surreptitious communication.)

Dance no more to their tricky,
Hypnotising drumbeats.
These are the promoters,
Indeed, the selfish perpetuators,
Of all the destructive practices
That characterise our landscape.
Endorse they the unsustainable methods
Of forest exploitation.
The soil depleting techniques
Of land cultivation....

(DRUMMERS sneak out in haste, letting their drums drop on to the ground with a crash. NDONGEBIDEMU and NTUNGWA dash out to chase after them, EYAMBE, TABI, EMANGA and MESAMBE following behind frantically.)

Don't, don't. Stop where you are.
Let them go, to return no more.
Get no closer to them.
Superbly charged
Are they at this instant,
And worse than a bonfire
Of evil and cruelty.
They are dangerous!
Very dangerous!
Let them go. Go! Go! Go!
And return no more!
No more! Return no more!

NDONGEBIDEMU, NTUNGWA, EYAMBE, TABI, EMANGA and MESAMBE reassemble around SANGU NGOE, panting heavily. Erie silence. Suddenly, they stand still, in various postures, staring at SANGU NGOE, spellbound. Then suddenly again they hold their hands in solidarity, forming a semi-circle that places SANGU NGOE at the centre, and then raise the hands up as a sign of victory.

GRADUAL FADEOUT

Thanks be to God